Original title:
The Fruit That Heals

Copyright © 2025 Creative Arts Management OÜ
All rights reserved.

Author: Cameron Blair
ISBN HARDBACK: 978-1-80586-421-9
ISBN PAPERBACK: 978-1-80586-893-4

Orchard's Embrace

In the orchard, apples play,
Dancing trees sway night and day.
Peaches laugh, all plump and round,
Chasing shadows on the ground.

Citrus giggles in the breeze,
Lemons chuckle, making tease.
Berries blush with fruity grace,
Nature's jest in every place.

Tokens of Nutritional Love

Bananas slip on sunny slides,
Pineapples wear their prickly hides.
Grapes compete in rolling race,
Juicy winners take their place.

Cherries play hide-and-seek, oh dear,
While kiwi's fuzzy charm draws near.
All these gifts in playful jest,
Serve up smiles, they do their best.

Journeys Through Sun-Drenched Orchards

A merry trip, the trees align,
Fruits parade, they sip on wine.
Raspberries whisper sweet, they tease,
Inviting snacks with charming ease.

Onward we stroll, in playful glee,
Peaches swing from bough to tree.
With each laugh, a treat to munch,
Nature's jest is our sweet lunch.

Invitations from Earth's Upside Down

In topsy-turvy lands so sweet,
Strawberries flip to greet your feet.
Berries bounce like jokers wild,
Each one plays the laughter's child.

Oranges slide on zesty wheels,
Making everyone spin on meals.
Mangoes waltz in golden chance,
Join the fruit in a merry dance.

Heartfelt Harvest

In a garden where laughter grows,
Tomatoes giggle as the breeze blows.
Pumpkins tell jokes, oh so delight,
Cucumbers grin under the moonlight.

Cherries dance, wearing a red hue,
Peas play hide and seek, it's true.
Eggplants wear hats, so very grand,
Squash makes mischief - isn't life planned?

Aromas of Alchemy

Onions cry, but in a funny way,
Garlic breath stinks, come what may.
Basil winks with a fragrant charm,
Thyme gives hugs, it's never harm!

Cinnamon sways to a jazzy beat,
Nutmeg's silly, can't take a seat.
With every flavor, fun's always near,
Spices in a dance - YAY! Let's cheer!

Reviving Roots

Carrots dig deep, avoid the light,
Beets wear capes, ready to take flight.
Radishes pout, but they wear a smile,
Turnips joke, make it all worthwhile.

Potatoes play tag buried in dirt,
Cauliflowers bloom, yet avoid the shirt.
Roots with giggles, growing unmasked,
Nature's odd comedy, who'd have asked?

Patience in the Peeling

Bananas boast, their peels so bright,
Yet slip on one? Oh! What a sight!
Avocados wait, a game of chance,
Ripening slowly, they join the dance.

Oranges roll, bursting with glee,
Lemons pucker, as sour as can be.
Each layer peeled, laughter is sealed,
In this fruity circus, joy's revealed!

Embers of Renewal Through Nature

In a grove where bananas giggle,
A pear with a wig starts to wiggle.
The apples wear shoes, a sight to behold,
They dance on the grass, all bright and bold.

Grapes throw a party, quite full of cheer,
Cherries suggest karaoke, loud and clear.
Melons in hats roll down the lane,
Spreading their joy, banishing pain.

With oranges juggling, all in a spin,
Lemons cracking jokes, let the fun begin!
Peaches play tag with giddy delight,
While limes whisper secrets, under moonlight.

So lend me your ear, gather around,
Nature's laughter in every sound.
With skills of the fruit, we're never alone,
Feeling so good, it's like coming home.

Vibrant Notes of Healing Harmony

In a jolly orchard, fruits all align,
Berries with banter, tasting divine.
Pineapples pirouette with fabulous flair,
While figs play chess without any care.

Watermelons chuckle, their seeds a wild game,
Citrus zest cheers, life's never the same.
The kiwi strums tunes on an orange's skin,
The rhythm of laughter, let the fun begin!

Tangerines tumble, they roll down the slope,
Playing hide-and-seek, spreading good hope.
Papayas gossip about fruit salad dreams,
Wishing for sunshine and laughter it seems.

So grab a ripe slice, let merriment grow,
The garden of joy puts on quite a show.
With every sweet bite, renew your delight,
Celebrating nature, from morning till night.

A Bowl of Nature's Gratitude

In a bowl bright and round,
Lies a gift from the ground.
With a wink and a jig,
It's a dance, not a fig.

Eating greens with delight,
As my stomach takes flight.
Cherries giggle and sway,
They're sweet, hip hooray!

Custodians of Nature's Goodness

We wear capes made of vines,
Saving snacks from the fines.
Bananas point with a laugh,
Saying, 'Joy is our path!'

Tomatoes in shades of red,
Stand guard in their bed.
Protecting each tasty bite,
With some veggie fight!

Flavorful Whispers of Health

Lemon zest sings a tune,
Making us dance like a loon.
Peaches chuckle and roll,
Tickling our health, that's the goal!

Each berry dons a crown,
Wearing smiles, never a frown.
Whispers of sweetness abound,
In each bite, laughter's found.

Health's Vibrant Tapestry

A salad of colors bright,
Gives our taste buds a fright!
Carrots vie for the crown,
While onions just drown!

The broccoli does a jig,
While cucumbers play big.
Each crunch, a comical cheer,
As veggies all disappear!

The Orchard's Secret

In the orchard of giggles, apples dance,
Their skins like smiles, in a fruity romance.
Bouncing berries in berry-tastic glee,
Who knew health could be this zany and free?

Citrus trees chuckle, lemons do a jig,
Lime slices slip, wearing their zesty wig.
Bananas with hats, oh what a sight!
Who knew fruits could host such a wild night?

Vitality's Palette

Paint me a canvas with colors so bright,
Carrots and peas in a veggie fight.
Spinach in capes, kale doing the twist,
Health in disguise? Well, how could we miss!

Grapes on a rollercoaster, round and round,
Pineapples bursting with laughter abound.
Mangoes in shades of sunset delight,
Nature's confetti, all says, "Take a bite!"

Song of Succulent Spirits

Peaches are plucking their sweet, fuzzy strings,
Melodies flowing on fuzzy plate swings.
Grapefruit crooning, a break from the norm,
Tangerines twirl, bringing zest to the form.

Cherries are gossiping, red as can be,
Dancing with mirth, as free as the sea.
Watermelons giggle, seeds fly like confetti,
All singing of joy, oh, aren't they ready?

Nature's Gentle Pledge

A promise unwrapped in a curly green vine,
Sassafras sprouting, fresh as a wine.
Carrots winking, doing the cha-cha,
Cucumbers chuckle, saying, "What's the fuss here?"

Radishes blush, with their tops held high,
Peppers are strutting, giving health a try.
Broccoli cheers, with a pop and a hop,
In this garden surprise, they'll all rise to the top!

Nature's Palette of Rejuvenation

In a garden where giggles bloom,
Elderberries dance, banishing gloom.
Lemons smile, with zesty flair,
Orange jokes fall through the air.

Mangoes sport a tropical grin,
While apples plot a juicy spin.
Bananas slip on sunny beams,
Making fruit salad the best of dreams.

Cherries chat with a cheerful laugh,
Pineapples tell a sweetened tale.
In this realm, all wear a crown,
Nature's jesters never frown!

Wholesome Wonders from the Tree

Peaches wiggle in playful strife,
While walnuts bring wisdom to life.
Grapes giggle as they tumble down,
Making juice that turns into crowns.

Kiwi whispers secrets of zest,
Cashews form a nutty quest.
Plums perform a juicy ballet,
In this orchard, they frolic and play.

Coconuts drop with a thump and cheer,
Squirrels scamper, no reason to fear.
Branch-bound laughter fills the air,
As each fruit jokes without a care.

Healing Currents of Orchard Gold

Berries beam with a wink and a sway,
Oranges giggle through their sunny display.
Avocados smirk, oh so divine,
While kumquats nudge, 'Let's intertwine!'

Pomegranates pop with a wink and roll,
Their seeds are tales of sweet control.
Figs are fascinated by their own fun,
Savoring laughter under the sun.

Papayas play peek-a-boo in the breeze,
Tickling tongues with flavors that tease.
In the orchard, joy knows no bounds,
Healing bursts are where laughter resounds.

Memoirs of a Sun-Laden Grove

In a sun-drenched orchard, stories unfold,
Where berries chatter and scents are bold.
Pears giggle as they dangle and sway,
Sharing the secrets of a sunny day.

Every banana knows its sweet spot,
With a punchline or two, they hit the jackpot.
Apples parade with crisp, quirky attire,
While grapefruit throws a zesty desire.

Citrus debates on who's the juiciest hit,
While a stubborn plum refuses to sit.
Together they laugh, like old friends in glee,
In this grove, they're the best company.

Pearls of Nourishing Delight

A berry burst upon my tongue,
Chasing blues that once were sung.
My salad's dancing on the plate,
With every bite, I celebrate!

Those citrus giggles share their zest,
In fruit bowl battles, who's the best?
A pear pranced in with style and grace,
While apple's got that sweet embrace!

Dancing in the Orchard's Light

Bananas swing with flair so bright,
While grapes roll in, what a sight!
The oranges juggle, oh what fun,
In this circus, all fruit's a pun!

With peaches winking, oh so sweet,
Even lemons tap their feet.
They twist, they shout, a fruity ball,
In this orchard, we've got it all!

Echoes of a Nutritious Legacy

Plums so juicy, they might burst,
In this giggle fest, they're the first!
Cherries wear a crown of cheer,
They all toast to the lively sphere!

Pineapples chuckle, standing tall,
While kiwi's got its fuzzy call.
For every slice, a crunch divine,
In this world, it's all so fine!

Gifts Beneath the Green Canopy

Under leaves where laughter reigns,
Where fruit rolls down like humorous trains.
Watermelon's chuckle is the best,
While berries whisper, 'Take a rest!'

In the shade, the flavors swell,
Each bite's a story, oh what a spell!
So grab your fork, let's have a feast,
In this garden, joy's released!

An Ode to Nature's Remedial Bounty

A berry sneezed, it made me laugh,
As if it knew it held the craft.
In its tiny skin, a jolly cheer,
I ate it up, called friends to steer.

An apple winked with rosy flair,
"Eat me up, lose your despair!"
I rolled my eyes, but took a bite,
My cold symptoms danced in flight.

The grape showed up with purple pride,
It claimed to cure my sleepy glide.
With every munch, my giggles grew,
It teased my taste buds, oh so true!

A citrus twist, a zesty grin,
It tickled right down to my chin.
With every squeeze, my worries flew,
Who needs a doctor? Not me, woo-hoo!

Flavorful Panacea

In the kitchen, fruits unite,
A medley bright, a woeful sight.
Bananas giggled, slipped around,
"Come try our magic, we astound!"

Mango danced with a sultry sway,
"Nectar sweet to chase the gray!"
I took a spoonful of this delight,
And suddenly my world felt bright.

Pineapple, king with a prickly crown,
Said, "Taste me if you wear a frown!"
It made my day, I shed my gloom,
A slice of sunshine in the room.

Kiwi winked, green fuzz galore,
"A twist of zest, crave us more!"
I laughed and tossed my cares away,
With every bite, I felt the play!

Essence of Healing Harvests

A cherry popped, like laughter spilled,
Its juicy power, quite fulfilled.
"A giggle here, a chuckle there!"
I felt the joy, just like a fair.

Lemon zipped with zesty zest,
"Sour power! I'm the best!"
It made me pucker, then I smiled,
Lemonade hugs, oh so wild.

A plum rolled in, a plump delight,
"Goodbye to woes, embrace the night!"
With every bite, I danced around,
Fruits of comedy, joy abounds.

Raspberries by the handful, bright,
Said, "Mirth is close; we'll take flight!"
Together laughter made us cheer,
Nature's mojos, always near!

Fruitful Serenade of Recovery

Under a tree, a fruit confab,
"Let's lift this mood, let's make it fab!"
Peaches joked, with fuzzy glee,
They whispered, "Cures? Just wait and see!"

A coconut said, "Don't take it slow,
Crack me open, watch the show!"
The milk inside brought laughter bright,
A silly sip to ease the night.

Oranges rolled in, bright and round,
"Citrus hugs, let joy abound!"
With a squirt, they danced around,
No frowns were left to be found.

Berry bandits, stealing smiles,
"We're the cure that lasts for miles!"
Each fruity joke, a playful tease,
Healing hearts with juicy ease!

Seeds of Renewal

In my garden, I found a pear,
It winked at me with flair.
Said, "Eat me up, don't be shy!"
I chuckled, wondering why.

A grape rolled by, took a seat,
Claimed he was a tasty treat.
With every giggle, fruit would squeeze,
Laughter sprouted like the trees.

An apple said, "I'm quite the wise,
With knowledge baked in every slice!"
Beneath the sun, we danced in glee,
Nature's laughs—and that's the key!

So if you hear a berry's grin,
Join the fun, let joy begin.
Each bite a laugh, a sweet delight,
Savor the giggles, feel just right!

Cascading Colors of Comfort

A lemon slipped on the kitchen floor,
Squeaked, "Watch out! I'm tangy for sure!"
A berry blushed, turned red with glee,
"You won't sour the party, trust me!"

Bananas laughed like silly clowns,
Peeling back their yellow gowns.
With colors bright, they danced around,
In fruity chaos, joy was found.

An orange shouted, "Let's make a jam!"
The berries cheered, "This is our plan!"
Spreading laughs like butter on bread,
With every taste, more joy spread.

So gather 'round, don't be shy,
For fruity fun can catch the eye.
In this vibrant, silly play,
Colors comfort, come what may!

Rejuvenating Nature's Palette

A peach proclaimed, "I'm ripe and fine,
Just one bite and you'll feel divine!"
A fruit basket threw a wild fest,
Each piece claiming it's the best!

Strawberries giggled, wearing caps,
Whispered secrets, gave high fives, perhaps?
Colorful antics made us cheer,
As apples rolled and joined the sphere.

Melons joked, "Cut me a slice,
My juicy heart is full of spice!"
In this patch, we had ourselves fun,
Raising sweetness under the sun.

So when life feels a tad too stale,
Grab a fruit, it'll never fail.
For every bite, a burst of glee,
Nature's palette sings, you'll see!

A Testament of Flavor and Life

A kiwi strutted with pride so bright,
"I'm fuzzy, fun, the best kind of bite!"
An orange chimed in, "Don't be too bold,
I'm sun-kissed sweet, worth more than gold!"

A bunch of bananas formed a line,
"We're here for laughs and jokes—divine!"
With every slip and silly trip,
Their playful dance began to zip.

Raspberries whispered, "Join the crew,
We've got the flavors and joy for you!"
In fruit's embrace, we felt the mirth,
A twist of humor, a burst of worth.

So savor each flavor life does lend,
With laughter and fun, around each bend.
In every bite, a story to show,
Love lives in fruit, and that's the glow!

Savoring the Earth's Embrace

In a grove where giants stand,
I ate a slice; it took my hand.
A juicy splat, oh what a mess,
Fruits in my hair, I must confess.

The laughter rang among the trees,
As pesky birds swung by with ease.
They squawked and swooped, what a delight,
Mocking my fruity, sticky plight.

Beneath the sun, I felt so free,
Green juices flowed like comedy.
I danced with glee, then slipped and fell,
A fruity patch turned out quite well!

With every bite, a giggle gained,
In nature's chaos, we're unchained.
Savoring joy, come join the fray,
In fruity games, we laugh and play.

Beneath the Canopy of Healing

Under leaves like umbrellas wide,
I found a treasure, oh, what pride!
A banana peel turned into a slide,
My graceful skills—I could not hide.

A pear rolled down with perfect flair,
Chased by squirrels, without a care.
We formed a team of fruity cheer,
I stifled laughs, then drew them near.

Nutty laughter filled the air,
As pockets burst with juicy fare.
I bit too hard, what a surprise,
The seeds launched forth like little spies!

Beneath this leafy, leafy dome,
I found the joys of nature's home.
A place where giggles bloom so bright,
Healing humor sparkles in the light.

Abundant Spheres of Vitality

Plump and round, the fruits were nice,
I tossed them high, a game of dice.
A watermelon smacked my friend,
And laughter echoed, no need to mend.

Grapes turned paintballs in our hands,
As we launched squishy fruity plans.
With every squish, a joyful shout,
Why chase our woes when it's this route?

Peaches slipped in joyful flings,
Like fruity darts on playful wings.
We giggled so, without a care,
As gooey goodness filled the air.

So join the fun with colors bright,
In nature's bowl, we laugh with might.
Abundant joy and laughter bloom,
In juicy chaos, we find our room.

Radiant Essence of Life

In a basket of wonder, colors blend,
A tangerine winks, a cheeky friend.
It rolled away, but I soon found,
A zesty chase on the grassy ground.

Strawberries giggled in playful rows,
Hiding beneath leaves like little pros.
I dove right in, a berry to catch,
A comical hunt, in nature's patch.

An orange bounced, a playful tease,
As lemons joined in on the breeze.
I laughed so hard, my belly shook,
As juicy tomfoolery overtook.

Oh, radiant essence, wild and free,
Life's punchlines ripening on the tree.
With every laugh, the heart ignites,
In a fruity world, joy takes flight.

Juicy Journeys of Resilience

In the garden where giggles roam,
Lemons dance wearing a zesty dome.
Bananas slip and take a leap,
While the apples giggle in a heap.

Cherries sing under skies so blue,
Mangoes plot in a fruity crew.
Pineapples wear crowns, oh so grand,
Planning a parade, quite unplanned!

Peaches waltz in summer's embrace,
While grapes juggle at a merry pace.
Oranges toss jokes like citrus seeds,
In this wacky world, laughter leads!

So raise a toast to nature's jest,
With every bite, we are truly blessed.
For through our laughter and fun,
We find resilience, second to none.

Resplendent Gifts from the Earth

Beneath the surface, gifts abound,
From tiny sprouts to sights profound.
Radishes sport a rosy hue,
Zucchini twirls, and beans they woo!

The carrots wear their orange coats,
While beets hum songs in high, sweet notes.
Potatoes chuckle in their soil,
With every laugh, they make us toil.

Spinach flexes with leafy flair,
Cabbages nag but always care.
As herbs gossip in fragrant tones,
They flavor friendships, never alone!

So let us share these earthy gifts,
And toast to nature's finest myths.
For in laughter and joy, we thrive,
Thanks to the bounty, we come alive!

Harvesting Life from Nature's Well

Rusty tractors rumble and start,
As pumpkins roll like works of art.
Kale struts by with leafy pride,
While carrots take a silly ride.

Corn on the cob tells goofy tales,
While cucumbers sport polka-dot scales.
Tomatoes wink with juicy charms,
And berries giggle on their farms.

Raspberries plotted a prank so sweet,
They tickle taste buds, can't be beat!
Their juicy jokes are never stale,
In this harvest, we shall prevail!

So gather round for nature's feast,
With humor's spice, our joy increased.
From fields to tables, laughter flows,
In every bite, the fun just grows!

Timeless Traditions of the Field

Under the sun where mischief smirks,
The fields are alive with playful quirks.
Squash tells tales of summers long,
While eggplants groove to nature's song.

Cucumbers chill, not a worry in sight,
While onions bask, shedding their light.
Garlic's punch brings laughter galore,
With every bite, we want more!

Radishes wiggle, trying to peek,
From the soil where they love to sneak.
Chives are whispering secrets low,
In this feast, we let our joy show!

So raise a fork to the fields so bright,
Where laughter waits, day and night.
In every nibble, a story unfolds,
Traditions of fun in veggies bold!

Gifts of the Good Earth

Beneath the tree, a treasure glows,
A wobbly pear, it brightly shows.
The squirrel slips, with a comic yelp,
As he plops right down, right on the kelp.

With juicy bites, the laughter spills,
And sticky fingers give us thrills.
A cherry bomb, oh what a sight,
Gather 'round and take a bite!

The pumpkins giggle, round and bright,
In funny hats, they dance at night.
When harvest comes, our skirts do twirl,
As veggies paint a merry whirl.

So grab a basket, join the cheer,
With every bite, we spread the cheer.
The good earth's gifts, both silly and sweet,
Bring joy and laughter in every treat.

Sweet Fragments of Wellness

A berry burst, oh what a tease,
Tiptoeing on vines, with grace and ease.
The raspberries chuckle, pink and bold,
While giggling tomatoes, shine like gold.

In the garden, whispers float,
'An apple a day? Just take notes!'
With every munch, our spirits rise,
As carrots dance in vibrant skies.

A lemon twist, with a wink and grin,
When life gives you zest, just dive on in!
We're sipping sunshine, with flair and fun,
While veggies play hide and seek in the sun.

So gather the harvest, don your hat,
Let's munch and crunch, and laugh a spat.
These sweet fragments, so bright and bold,
Are the secrets to health, worth their weight in gold!

Nature's Abundant Remedies

In the orchard, laughter sings,
As apples dance on bouncy swings.
With every crunch, a giggle flies,
As nature's waltz makes silly ties.

A cucumber winks, sly as a fox,
While celery sticks tell carrot knocks.
The kale wears shades, looking so chic,
In the garden party, all stars they speak.

Banana peels, with comedic flair,
Slip underfoot, we gasp, we stare!
Laughter erupts, as we take a spill,
In this garden, joy's the main bill.

With hugs of sunshine, vines entwine,
Nature's remedies are simply divine.
So munch away, let giggles reign,
In this patch of laughter, there's no pain!

Chasing Sunshine Among the Branches

Up in the trees, the lemons hide,
With playful glee, they bounce and glide.
A swing on a branch, a peach takes flight,
As the cherries cheer in the golden light.

Our picnic basket held with flair,
Strawberries wearing crowns, so rare.
Mangoes wink, with a juicy grin,
Chasing sunshine with every spin.

The grapes are gossiping, full of zest,
While pomegranates look sharp, the best-dressed.
Each fruit a jester, bringing delight,
As we laugh in the warm sunlight.

So let's frolic beneath leafy green,
With nature's bounty, all the fun's seen.
Chasing sunshine, let's make it clear,
These fruity friends bring laughter near!

Serenade of Spheres

In a garden of laughter, where apples tease,
A pear tells a joke that brings you to your knees.
Bananas giggle as they slip and slide,
While berries burst forth in a colorful ride.

A mango struts in, feeling oh so bright,
Winking and twisting, a true daytime delight.
Pineapples prance with crowns on their heads,
Dancing with passion, no worries, no threads.

Oranges boast tanginess, a zest for the game,
They laugh at the lemons, who don't feel the same.
Together they form a jovial crew,
In this comical fruit world, it's all about you!

So grab a cheeky slice or a juicy squirt,
Join the fruit party, wear happiness like a shirt.
In this fun-filled orchard, joy takes its stand,
With giggles aplenty, the best fruit band.

Rebirth in Orchards

Once a sad slice of green, now a vibrant red,
The tomato chuckles, saying, 'Look where I've tread!'
With basil beside, they whirl and twirl,
Laughing at the spinach, who just gives a whirl.

Citrus fruits gather, a zesty parade,
Limes spin around, in a green masquerade.
Grapes form a cluster, so tight and so sweet,
It's a grape vine jig on a fruity retreat!

Pomegranates burst forth like ticking time bombs,
Seeds flying everywhere, causing fruit-ful qualms.
'Catch me if you can!' the cherries will shout,
As they roll down the hill, giggling all about.

So, if you feel sour, just give it a try,
Join the fun orchard, let laughter fly high.
With every bite, a giggle will sprout,
In this merry grove, joy's what it's about!

The Healing Orchard's Song

In a grove so sunny, fruits start to sing,
Melody sweet, what joy do they bring!
Plums pluck the strings while peaches hum along,
Creating a chorus, a berry-licious song.

Coconuts sway with a rhythm quite bold,
While cherries cheer on, their laughter untold.
Mangoes take solos, full of sweet flair,
Even grumpy old lemons can't help but care!

'Let's dance!' cries the fig, in a suit of deep brown,
While everyone prances, there's no need to frown.
Each fruit has a role, in this silly affair,
Together they bloom, bringing joy to the air.

So come join the chorus, be part of the scene,
With laughter and sweetness, it's a fruity routine.
In this whimsical orchard, life takes a spin,
With each juicy note, let the fun begin!

Juicy Resurrection

Once a forgotten orange, shriveled and gray,
Found new life in laughter, hip-hip-hooray!
Banana slipped by, in a zany old suit,
Together they danced, two fruits so astute.

'Look at me now,' cried the radiant peach,
'With fuzz like a cloud, I'm within reach!'
Kiwis in shades, shaking up the scene,
Said, 'Life's a smoothie, let's make it serene!'

Fig rolls his eyes, thinking, 'What a charade!'
But suddenly chuckled, feeling the cascade.
Cantaloupe giggled, a sweet, rounded sphere,
As they all cheered for the peaches who cheer!

So let go of the past, be fruity and bold,
In this wacky orchard, watch stories unfold.
With every ripe moment, laughter ignites,
In a juicy rebirth, let's all reach new heights!

Sweet Nectar of Renewal

In a garden green and bright,
Mangoes dance in warm sunlight.
Bananas giggle, what a sight!
They slip and slide, pure delight.

Apples claim they're health's best friend,
While silly pears just pretend.
With every bite, giggles blend,
Nature's remedy, we commend!

Juicy berries burst and grow,
Tickling taste buds down below.
Lemons frown, but can't say no,
To laughter's echo, in a row!

With every crunch, we heal and munch,
In this feast, we laugh and crunch.
Forget the doc, let's pack a lunch,
Of fruity fun, and joy to hunch!

Nature's Healing Harvest

Watermelons wear their green hats,
Cracking jokes with chubby chats.
Cherries giggle in sweet spats,
Dancing round in happy flats.

Peaches blush in summer's breeze,
As oranges joke, "No one sees!"
With puns and smiles, they bring ease,
To grumpy faces, just like peas!

Grapes roll by in silly pairs,
Telling tales of juicy flares.
With laughter shared, no one cares,
For all our troubles, fruit bears!

Even coconuts crack a grin,
As they say, "Don't let them in!"
Put worries aside, let the fun begin,
With nature's joy, we always win!

Orchard of Whispers

In the orchard, secrets grow,
Fruits giggle in a row.
Ripe figs whisper soft and low,
"Join us for a fruity show!"

Plums tell tales of summer dreams,
While zestful limes plot sweet schemes.
With laughter flowing like sunbeams,
Together we burst at the seams!

Strawberries blush, a rosy hue,
As raspberries cheer with a hearty crew.
We nibble in a joyful queue,
Nature's punchline, always true!

So gather round, let's have a feast,
As fruits unite, our joys released.
Laughter shared, a perfect beast,
In whispers sweet, our hearts increased!

Bounty of Breath

A basket brimming, all aglow,
Fruit in hand, let the laughter flow.
With zesty bites, we steal the show,
In every crunch, our spirits grow!

Pineapples beam with sunny glee,
While kiwi hides, peeking free.
"Join the fun," they laugh with me,
In this fruity jubilee!

Blackberries chuckle in small bites,
Tangled giggles in summer nights.
Holding secrets that ignite,
The joys of life, oh what a sight!

Peanuts join, but they're a mess,
As juicy fruits bring happiness.
Each little snack, a soft caress,
In nature's lap, we feel so blessed!

Glistening Beads of Vitality

In the orchard, colors burst,
Fruit laughs as they quench your thirst.
One cheeky apple starts to sway,
Says, 'Eat me first, I save the day!'

Bananas take a slippery slide,
While oranges jive with juicy pride.
A raisin whispers, 'I'm not old,
Just dried and wise, a story told!'

Strawberries wear a crown of cream,
They giggle and swirl in a dream.
Each slice a funny little tease,
'Come share the joy, oh, please, oh, please!'

In this garden, laughter shines,
With every bite, a punchline whines.
So grab a bowl, let whimsy flow,
These glistening beads put on a show!

Blossoms of Nourishing Care

In the kitchen, chaos reigns,
Lettuce winks and cabbage gains.
Broccoli dons its green attire,
Says, 'I'm the one you should admire!'

Tomatoes roll and try to race,
They tumble down, a fun embrace.
A carrot giggles in the pot,
'I'm sweet and crunchy—give it a shot!'

Peas in pods, they chat and roll,
'We're not just sidekicks, we play a role!'
A radish blushes all in red,
'Just pick me first and I'll be fed!'

In this salad, tales unfold,
With each bite, new laughter told.
Nature's humor, bright and rare,
In blossoms bold, we all take care!

Serenade of Recovery in Bloom

In the garden, laughter grows,
Peppers dance, and the spinach glows.
A merry melon swings on high,
It sings, 'I'm sweet, just give me a try!'

With a kiwi's fuzzy, funky flair,
'Come taste my magic, if you dare!'
Lettuce joins with a crunchy beat,
Making every meal feel like a treat.

Onions cry, but make it fun,
'I bring tears, but I'm number one!'
Cherries giggle, in a clump,
'We're bittersweet; come join the jump!'

Thus, the garden hums a tune,
Of recovery under the moon.
Each bite brings smiles, a cheer in bloom,
A woven melody to chase the gloom!

Conversations Among the Trees

Under branches, secrets trade,
Apples whisper, 'Don't be afraid!'
The pears giggle, swinging bright,
'We're here to bring some pure delight!'

Citrus fruits hold lively chats,
'Zest is best; imagine that!'
Peaches share their fuzzy fuzz,
In every bite, a joyful buzz.

Cherries gossip, all in red,
'Life is sweeter, just like bread!'
A mango jumps, with flair it brings,
'In my world, everyone sings!'

So gather 'round this fruity crew,
In conversations, laughter grew.
Among the trees, the stories play,
In nature's humor, we find our way!

Elixir of the Orchard

In the orchard, apples laugh,
Fruits disguised, a clever craft.
Bananas slip, they make us slide,
Grapes in bunches, our silly pride.

Cherries dance, they twirl and spin,
Peaches blush, a fruity grin.
Pineapples wear a prickly crown,
Juicy antics, they won't frown.

Mangoes wink, their golden glow,
Lemons pucker, but still they flow.
Oranges juggle, zest on display,
In this fruit fest, we laugh and play.

So join the fun on this wild spree,
Nature's bounty, oh so free.
When life gets tough, just take a bite,
These jolly gems make everything right.

Sweet Remedies from the Garden

In the garden, laughter grows,
Carrots hide, in silly shows.
Cabbages wear hats in the dirt,
They giggle soft, never hurt.

Tomatoes blush, a saucy flare,
Herbs whisper secrets, fresh air.
Zucchinis hide, in plain sight,
Garden tricks inspire delight.

Peas in pods, they pop like cheer,
Radishes joke, but oh so dear.
Lettuce grins, a leafy throne,
Their leafy jokes, all their own.

Sweet remedies for every plight,
Nature's humor, pure delight.
So harvest laughter, take a card,
In this garden, joy's not hard.

Parables of Harvest's Touch

Once a berry told a tale,
Of a pumpkin dressed, a splendid whale.
Strawberries giggled, berries bright,
In the field, they spread delight.

Tomatoes sang of sunny days,
Corn gave speeches, in funny ways.
Wheat wore shoes, danced about,
Nature's secrets, we laugh, no doubt.

A curious squash began to jest,
"Why did the carrot never rest?"
Broccoli chuckled, green and wise,
"You'll find your laughs beneath the skies!"

So harvest stories, share the fun,
Nature's humor, for everyone.
In this parable, let's rejoice,
Finding laughter in nature's voice.

Nectar of Renewal

In the field, sweet nectar flows,
Buzzing bees with silly toes.
Honeyed laughter, drips and glows,
Life's a feast, as nature knows.

The flowers giggle, sunbeams tease,
With every breeze, they dance with ease.
Bees wear shades, they're on a roll,
Sipping nectar, that's their goal.

Berry smoothies in the sun,
Mixing joy, and oh what fun!
Mint leaves join in silly dance,
Giving every sip a chance.

So let's toast to nature's brew,
A cup of laughter, tried and true.
When life feels tough, don't be afraid,
Sip this nectar, joy remade.

Berries of Redemption

In the fridge, a berry pile,
Naughty sweets with cheeky style,
One blue, one red, oh what a scene,
They dance around, looking quite mean.

They whisper low, 'Give us a try!'
Pancakes blush, the syrup sighs,
With every bite, the giggles start,
These fruity pals are quite the art.

Sticky fingers, laughter spreads,
Mismatched colors, straws in beds,
Grapes that roll and tumble loud,
Unruly snacks that make us proud.

No need for doctors, no need for pills,
Just a bowl of cherries fills the thrills,
With every taste, we lift our glee,
Who knew that fruit could set us free?

An Offering in Every Bough

Under branches, apples giggle,
With tiny worms that dance and wriggle,
Each bite's a crunch, a tart surprise,
They drop and roll, oh how time flies!

Pears wear hats made out of leaves,
Chasing ants, inventing thieves,
'Look at us!' they proudly boast,
In this orchard, we raise a toast.

Bananas slip, it's quite a show,
They knock us down, we laugh and glow,
A smoothie circus, rhythm and rhyme,
In every inch, there's fun to find.

The fruit-stand jester, plump and bold,
Hiding secrets, stories untold,
With every bite, a laugh takes flight,
Nature's joy, served up just right.

Melody of Rich Flavors

Mangoes croon in the summer sun,
While peaches dance, oh isn't it fun?
Strawberries strut with a jazzy flair,
Their sweet serenades fill the air.

Citrus zings with a zesty cheer,
Lemon's punch brings the folks near,
Limes roll in like a little tease,
With every slice, the giggles squeeze.

Grapefruit's wink joins the silly tune,
Rotating like astronauts to the moon,
A fruity band, so chic and spry,
In the concert of taste, we can't deny.

Their juicy notes, a tasty spree,
Every bite's a melody, full of glee,
In the bowl, they gather and play,
Sticky fingers, the sweetest ballet.

Life's Succulent Remedies

Kiwi jokes with a fuzzy skin,
'Taste my sweetness, let's begin!'
Peeling layers, laughter flows,
In the bowl, funny chaos grows.

Oranges giggle, a citrus fight,
'Who will brighten the dullest night?'
Slices flying, juice on the floor,
Every chuckle opens a door.

Avocados mash into a spree,
'Who's the guac? Come dance with me!'
They spread the joy on each crisp chip,
Leaping high on this flavor trip.

In fruit's embrace, we celebrate,
Life's little quirks we cultivate,
With every crunch, our woes decline,
In this platter, flavors align.

Elixir From the Grove

In a garden where giggles grow,
I found a berry with quite the glow.
It promised joy in every bite,
But made me dance through the night!

A citrus twist, oh what a treat,
It tickled my tongue and made me tweet.
Friends joined in with snickers loud,
As we pranced like a merry crowd.

Bananas slipped, oh what a fuss,
My dance moves turned to a comic plus.
With every bite, laughter would rise,
Like bubbles of joy in sunny skies.

In this grove of healing cheer,
Happiness sprouted, far and near.
With each morsel, the world feels right,
So let's feast, it's a laugh-out-loud night!

Seeds of Restoration

Planted seeds of silly mirth,
Took a dive for all they're worth.
One sprouted legs, what a sight,
Told me jokes until the night!

A watermelon, round and bright,
Wore a hat, oh what a fright!
It whispered secrets, juicy and crude,
Made me chuckle, brightened my mood.

Grapes rolled around, they had a ball,
Told me tales of the garden haul.
With every punchline, they fermented glee,
A vineyard of joy, can't you see?

With each seed that burst with fun,
My laughter echoed, began a run.
Restoration found in every bite,
When food is funny, it feels just right!

Ripened Remedies

An apple a day kept the doctor away,
But a fig turned out to be the play.
With squishy delight, it showed me how,
To turn my frown into a wow!

Peaches with giggles, so absurd,
They chatted and gossiped, oh what a word!
With every nibble, my heart felt light,
These ripened gems brought silly delight.

A pomegranate burst, seeds flew like stars,
I laughed so hard, it shook the jars.
Juicy tales spilled from its core,
A remedy that left me wanting more!

These treasures of nature bring joy anew,
With flavors that dance and tickle too.
In every bite, a quick remedy found,
With laughter and smiles, our souls unbound!

Serene Succulence

In a bowl of bright things, sat a peach,
I took a bite, what a colorful reach!
It giggled and jiggled, full of cheer,
Made my worries simply disappear.

Mangoes wearing sunglasses so cool,
Taught me laughter is a golden rule.
They tangoed and twirled in the sun,
With every slice, joy had begun.

Pineapple crowns bobbed like kings,
Charmed my heart with their silly flings.
Caught in a riddle, their sweetness soared,
A riot of laughter and smiles adored.

So let's gather fruits, both funny and bright,
In this garden of joy, we'll take flight.
Serene moments with every taste,
In a fruity world, there's no room for haste!

Elixirs Wrapped in Color

In a garden where laughter grows,
Bananas wearing silly clothes.
Cherries giggle with a splash,
While lemons dance in a bright green sash.

Mangoes rolling, quite the sight,
Flirting fiercely from left to right.
Limes tell jokes, oh so tart,
Creating giggles, a fruity art.

Peaches prance in a swirling spree,
Tickling each other, it's quite a spree.
Coconuts chuckle, split their shells,
Exchanging secrets, oh, fruity spells!

So pick your potion, a vibrant cheer,
In this medley of joy, there's nothing to fear.
For every bite, a funny surprise,
Wrapped in colors that tantalize!

Bounty of Seasons Past

Autumn leaves in a vibrant mess,
Cider apples in fancy dress.
Pineapples toss their terrible hair,
While pumpkins giggle, so round and fair.

Berries bumble and buzz around,
Whispering secrets, making their sound.
A kiwi slips with a playful grin,
Right into a bowl where the fun begins!

Nuts in coats of fuzzy delight,
Put on a show every single night.
With every nibble, laughter pours,
In this bounty, the joy restores!

So grab your basket, a silly chase,
Tasting goodness in every place.
The harvest sings, so bright and bold,
A laughter-filled tale that's always told!

Radiance in Every Harvest

In orchards where sunlight plays,
Oranges juggle in joyful ways.
Apples twirl in vibrant cheer,
Winking whispers, "Come over here!"

Grapes bounce high, a bouncy crew,
Wearing smiles in every hue.
Watermelon makes a silly face,
Giggles shared in a friendly space.

Strawberries giggle in their patch,
Each berry ready to make a match.
Chilled fruit punch in a frosty mug,
A party starts with a happy shrug!

So join the harvest, come take part,
With every taste, you'll feel the heart.
Radiance shines from every bite,
As flavors twirl in pure delight!

Aromas of Wholesomeness

In kitchens where scents intertwine,
Peppers prance like they're on a line.
Garlic giggles with spicy flair,
Singing savory songs in the air.

Basil winks with a mischievous toss,
While onions play, playing the boss.
Cinnamon's twirl, a fragrant dance,
Invites the apples to join in the chance.

Honey drips like a golden stream,
Creating sweet moments that brightly beam.
Tomatoes joke, a juicy bunch,
In this kitchen, we're having lunch!

So come and feast, laughter will bloom,
As aromas rise, chase away gloom.
With every dish, a hearty cheer,
Food's magic brings the joy near!

Fragrant Solstice

In the garden, a berry danced,
With a wiggle and jiggle, it pranced.
Said, "I'm sweet, not a chore!"
And made everyone want more.

An apple claimed it had charm,
While pear tried to sound the alarm!
But the cherry burst forth with flair,
"I'm the best! Just stop and stare!"

A lemon laughed, oh so bright,
"I'm sour, but still feel just right!"
While grapes spilled their laughs in a cup,
"Come on, join us! Don't eat alone, gulp!"

So gather close, let's all cheer,
For fruity fun, there's nothing to fear!
In this world of color and taste,
Life's too short, don't let it go to waste!

Vital Nectar

In a grove where the bees took flight,
A tub of honey gleamed so bright.
"Just one scoop and you'll see,
I'm the antidote to your glee!"

Along came a mango, smooth and bold,
"I'm sweet enough! I shouldn't be sold!"
While papaya teased with a wink,
"I'll be your drink! Just take a sip and think!"

Pineapple showed off its tropical pride,
"Slice me up! Let's take a ride!"
While kiwi laughed, all fuzzy and shy,
"Combined, we make health soar high!"

A cocktail mixer swirled in delight,
With fruit confetti all shining bright.
Let's blend these wonders, let's have some fun,
For laughter and health, we all have won!

Colors of Cure

There's a rainbow in the kitchen drawer,
With veggies and fruits that you can't ignore.
Carrots sang, "We're the vision team!"
While broccoli said, "We reign supreme!"

Tomatoes blushed deep, red and bold,
"A dash of me? I'm worth more than gold!"
And cucumbers whispered, cool as a breeze,
"Chop me up... I'll bring you ease!"

Avocados creamed out, all green and chic,
"Spread me on toast, I'm the health freak!"
While bell peppers shouted, all colors on show,
"In stir-fry, we'll make that flavor blow!"

So grab your colors, mix with delight,
Each bite is a party, a dazzling sight!
Together they laughed, a colorful crew,
Making health fun, just for you!

Lush Sanctuary

In a jungle where coconuts sway,
A party began at the close of the day.
"Let's explore!" the pineapple cried,
"I've got the juice! Come, take a ride!"

A passion fruit winked, coy and fun,
"With my seeds, who needs a gun?"
While bananas slipped, oh what a sight,
"Peel and reveal, I'm pure delight!"

Kiwi kids played hide and seek,
"I'm fuzzy, but I'm not unique!"
As berries burst in tales of cheer,
"Join our feast, the end is near!"

Let's dance in this lush paradise,
Where laughter echoes like sweet advice.
So, grab your fruit, let humor flow,
In this sanctuary, we're all aglow!

www.ingramcontent.com/pod-product-compliance
Lightning Source LLC
Chambersburg PA
CBHW070332120526
44590CB00017B/2853